Anthony Ritthaler

Escaping Depression

A Book Of Hope, Help and Healing

PUBLISHED by PARABLES
Earthly Stories with a Heavenly Meaning

ANTHONY RITTHALER

Pathways To The Past

Each volume stands alone as an Individual Book
Each volume stands together with others
to enhance the value of your collection

Build your Personal, Pastoral or Church Library
Pathways To The Past contains an ever-expanding list of
Christendom's most influencial authors

Augustine of Hippo
Athanasius
E. M. Bounds
John Bunyan
Brother Lawrence
Jessie Penn-Lewis
Bernard of Clairvaux
Andrew Murray
Watchman Nee
Arthur W. Pink
Hannah Whitall Smith
R. A. Torrey
A. W. Tozer
Jean-Pierre de Caussade
Thomas Watson
And many, many more.

Escaping Depression
Anthony Ritthaler
Rights: All Rights Reserved
ISBN 978-1-945698-36-1
Doctrinal theology, Inspiration
Salvation, Meditation
Other books by this author include: Walking On The Water With Jesus (Volume 1 and 2), Soaring With Eagles (Volume 1 and 2), Roaring At The Enemy and A Devil From The Beginning.

Cover Design by Fury Cover Design
www.furycoverdesign.com

Anthony Ritthaler

Escaping Depression

A Book Of Hope, Help and Healing

PUBLISHED by PARABLES
Earthly Stories with a Heavenly Meaning

Tony's Words Of Freedom, Strength and Power

"When we choose to dwell in the dark, depression will come and leave its mark."

"DEPRESSION:
D = Drains
E = Everything
P = Physically,
R = Religiously,
E = Emotionally,
S = Spiritually,
S = Socially,
I = Inwardly,
O = Outwardly,
N = Nonstop."

"Depression can rob us of our present and future while it haunts us with our past."

"When depression captures your mind mentally, it will cause you to want to give up physically."

Escaping Depression

"Run from the dark, and step into the light and depression with scatter in absolute fright."

"When you are in depression you will feel all alone, but remember there is always hope at the foot of God's throne."

"If the Devil can get you depressed he knows you will have no ability to rest."

"When the Devil has you depressed, come and lean on Jesus' breasts."

"If Satan can cause you to mope, it won't be long until you will feel like you're at the end of life's rope."

"When depression has you down, take your battle to higher ground."

"If you choose to be depressed, you will always have great stress, but if you will choose to let it go the glory will begin to flow."

"Depression is Satan's prison, but thank God Christ has risen."

"Don't let depression rob you of your dreams, come to Jesus and find out what living really means."

"When Satan runs your mind through mud, there is a fountain filled with blood."

"The battle of depression starts in the mind, if we get that right we will be alright."

"Depression can leave us in defeat, but victory is found at Jesus' feet."

"When we allow depression to keep us in chains the Glory of God will just pass us by and we will never know what it's like to fly."

"Spread your wings and soar and your depression will be no more."

"The blood of Jesus can set you free, and depression will have no choice but to flee."

"Depression will cause you to suffer great loss, but all is forgiven at the old rugged cross."

"Depression will drive you insane, but God's word will make everything plain."

"When you're staring in the face of depression, go to God's throne for a prayer session."

"When depression attacks your soul, remember thy faith shall make thee whole."

"When the Devil sends attacks on every side, run to Christ and under His wing you can hide."

Table of Contents

Tony's Words Of Freedom, Strength and Power
Special Thanks
Introduction
1. What Depression Did To Me
2. What Depression Has Done To Others
3. What Depression Will Do To You
4. When Depression Hits You, Run to Godly Music As Quick As You Can
5. If You Wish to Escape Depression, Run Away From Temporal Things, and Run Towards Eternal Things
6. When You Feel Depressed, Help Others
7. When Depression Takes Over Pray, Pray, and Pray Some More
8. In Order To Get Out of Depression, We Must Leave the Darkness and Step into the Light
9. If You Feel Like You Can't Escape Depression, Run to Praise and Worship
10. When Depression Is Near, Run to God's House
11. When You're Battling Depression, Run Towards Positive Thinking
12. If You Are in Depression, Run Towards Joy Whatever the Cost
13. When Depression Strikes, It's Wise to Run to God's Throne

14. Run to the Prince of Peace When You Can't Get a Handle on Depression
15. Run Towards a Forgiving Spirit and You Can Get Out of Depression
16. When You Are Depressed, Run to the History Books For Help
17. Run Towards A New Beginning and Away From a Guilty Conscience and Depression Can Be Removed
18. You Must Run to Total Faith If You Want Depression to be Taken Care Of
19. Whenever You Are Depressed, Deep Bible Study Works
20. Live A Busy and Productive Life and You Can Cut Down Depression
21. If You Are in Depression, Run Towards Spirit-Filled Preaching
22. Run Towards Positive People When You Are Depressed
23. When Depression Hits You, Drop What You're Doing and Run to the Blood of Jesus
24. Conclusion

Special Thanks

I'm extremely thankful for the many different categories of people God uses to help us get out of depression and I would like to personally thank a few of them now.

First of all, I would like to thank all Godly singers who are used to uplift our spirits through song. Without the ministry of music life would be such a drag, and if God is using your music to speak to others I want to say thank you from the depths of my soul. Christian music has been very instrumental in bringing me out of depression and without Godly music there is no way on earth I would be an author today. Whenever Satan seeks to discourage me I often run to Christian music for a refreshing, and it has been a refuge for me in my walk with God. Thanks singers, song writers, and anyone who serves in this manner.

Another category of people I would love to thank are encouragers. This world is in desperate need of more like you, who go the extra mile to help others achieve their goals. With this type of book I needed encouragers not discouragers because the fight from Satan himself was very real. Thank you for your kind words, support, and prayer, it means the world to me. If you are an encourager I thank you for your ministry.

Last of all I would like to thank God-called men of God all over this world. Thanks for your faithfulness, your hard work, and for the vital part you play in getting folks out of depression. Heaven only knows how many you have touched through your ministries, and I know in my heart I would still be wallowing in depression if not for a few Spirit-filled preachers that God sent my way. Your labor has not gone unnoticed by our Savior, and without your submission to the Lord I fear what this world would be. Keep on keeping on in your fight towards righteousness, and thank you so much for your love for others.

I wish to close out this special thanks by thanking my great Savior, the Lord, Jesus Christ, for all His guidance and help with this book. Without the Spirit of God helping me none of this is possible. Thank you Lord for your mercy, grace, and love that has sheltered me every step of the way, and thanks to everyone else that helped in any way to make this come to pass.

With Love,
Bro Tony

Introduction

Depression is real, it's dangerous, and it is growing more and more with each passing day. All across this world people are losing their joy, peace, and purpose for living and Satan is loving every minute of it. Depression has the ability to damage, hurt, and destroy our will to live and it will keep our minds in a state of torture if we let it. Whenever we are in the dark prison of depression we will never be productive and we will never bring glory to our Lord, Jesus Christ. Depression can strike any caliber of person and it never asks for permission. When it strikes we must be ready to fight it off with everything we have or we will be miserable day in and day out. Some of the greatest people who ever lived battled with depression and no one is immune to it hitting them at different times in their life. Once Satan can get someone to dwell in deep valleys of depression, he is a master at squeezing the life out of them through lies and deception. The Bible says that Satan can keep people captive at his own will. The Devil's number one trick that he uses on those in depression is convincing them that they are alone and nobody cares. Satan uses guilt, lies, confusion, and deception to isolate people and once he toys with the mind it will be an uphill battle from there. Suicide is rising every year and depression is the major reason why. Always remember everything Satan whispers is a lie and his ultimate goal is to keep you in chains of misery and despair. The longer he can succeed in keeping you depressed the more he enjoys it. Satan loves to keep people paralyzed by fear and during these times of trials he will try to tell you it's hopeless so you might as well give up.

Let me give you this verse of encouragement found in I Corinthians 10:13 "No matter how dark your valley may be always understand that God has offered you a way to escape if we will exit through the avenues He provides". I Corinthians 10:13 says "There hath no temptation taken you but such as is common to man: but God is faithful who will not suffer you to be tempted above that ye are able; but will with the temptation also make a way to escape that ye may be able to bear it". There is good news my friends: God is still in the business of restoring minds, hearts, and lives for His glory. There is freedom in Christ and He has the ability to break every mental chain that binds us. The Bible says in Hebrews 2:14-15 "For as much as the children are partakers of flesh and blood, he also himself likewise took part of the same, that through fear of death he might destroy him that had the power of death, that is the Devil; and deliver them who through fear of death were all their lifetime subject to bondage". There is liberty, victory, and freedom in the Lord and the Bible says He will never leave us nor forsake us. No matter what battle you are facing there is sweet peace in Christ.

The Word of God gives us many different avenues we can run to when depression hits us and if we will run to these avenues we will begin to bathe in the sunshine of his love again. In this book I will list 20 things that will help you overcome depression and I pray to God you will find joy again. Refuse to listen to Satan's lies another day, rise up in victory, and free yourself form the torments of depression. Life is too short and God is too great for you to live beneath your worth. Take heed to these 20 avenues and experience power like you have never known before. Enjoy the book everyone.

Itroduction Scriptures

I Corinthians 10:13: There hath no temptation taken you but such is common to man: but God is faithful who will not suffer you to be tempted above that ye are able; but will with the temptation also make a way to escape that ye may be able to bear it.

I John 2:14-15: For as much as the children are partakers of flesh and blood, he also took part of the same, that through fear of death he might destroy him that had the power of death, that is the Devil; and deliver them who through fear of death were all their lifetime subject to bondage.

Chapter One

What Depression Did To Me

When I was 20 years old, I went through a deep depression that lasted for 20 months and it nearly killed me on several occasions. The words I would use to describe this time in my life was brutal, miserable, and lonely. Nothing I did would help, and every day was an absolute struggle. Many thoughts of suicide raced through my mind, and every waking moment I felt trapped in the prison of my thoughts. My joy left me, and my desire to depart was greater than my desire to stay. Every single day I would cry so hard that my strength would leave me and I could barely stand. All throughout the day the Devil would replay the same doubts and questions in my mind and it got to the point of me nearly giving up all hope. I felt hopeless, alone, defeated, and my peace and ability to think properly was completely gone. All I wanted to do was sleep and being in depression took more energy from me than playing basketball for 8 hours would. People thought I was crazy, and I started to as well.

During this time in my life I lost my zest for life and I hated to go out in public. There were no friends to comfort me, no song in my heart, and the Devil confused my mind and stole so much from me. Often I would break out in cold sweats and collapse to the ground. It felt like I was carrying a thousand pound weight around my neck at all times, and to be alone was my greatest desire. Often I would look out the window and watch the world race by and tears would fill my eyes because I had no intentions to join them. In days gone by sports were my haven and they were always something that made me happy but during these dark times of my life sports did not help. When I went to church I would watch others shout and all I wanted to do was to go home so I could be alone in my thoughts. My life was filled with shame, confusion, sadness, and misery, and nothing seemed to comfort me. Days felt like nights, and nights never ended. I was defeated, heart broken, weak, fragile, and needy in every way. For a long time I felt like I was destined for disaster and I had no answers. My will to live was almost gone and I almost gave up on life. On the inside I felt like a ticking time bomb, and on the outside I looked like death warmed over.

All throughout these 20 months of depression I pushed myself to God's house despite how I felt and that eventually was the key to getting out of my dungeon of depression. When I was going through this war of depression I refused to go to drugs for quick fixes because I was taught that if I trusted God, He could set me on a solid rock, so I held on with all I had. When hope seemed all gone, help was on the way and in a revival meeting at my lowest point God sent a Spirit-filled preacher that was instrumental in getting me out of depression. As he preached that night I felt a power sweep over me that hadn't been there in so long and I hung on every word he said. The Spirit of God got a hold of me that night and tears of misery turned into tears of joy as I felt the chains of depression breaking one at a time. My energy returned, and so did my joy and I went to the altar and asked God to use me and take away the dark cloud that hung over me. God answered this prayer from my heart and shortly after that night I started investing in the ministry of God every day of my life. God renewed my mind, healed my heart, and dumped His blessing bucket all over me. Now by the grace of Almighty God, the Lord has given me a wife, a child, a home, and joy unspeakable and full of glory. Every day is fresh and new and His power is felt on a daily basis.

Jesus is able to break any chain that binds us and my life is living proof. God has allowed me to write 8 books, go on 23 radio shows, and help preachers all over the world. The Lord took this broken vessel and He is forming me into His vessel and He can do the same for you. If you feel like giving up, always remember that Jesus can take your broken pieces and make you into something beautiful. Depression nearly claimed my life and I am writing this book to give people hope. If God can salvage me, He can salvage you too. A great man of God said one time concerning his life, and I quote "Satan had a plan, but God had a greater plan. For over 15 years God has allowed me to walk in victory and joy and I never want to go back to the days of depression again". Without God we are nothing, but through His Spirit He has given us everything. Trust me, I know how powerful depression can be and it nearly destroyed my life. I'm thankful every day for God's mercy in my life and I desire for you to gain help through the pages to come. Never give up on hope, and never be afraid to run to Jesus. He can weather any storm that comes our way. Thank you Lord for pulling me out of that horrible pit and I pray you do the same for all who desire to escape its torments.

Thanks be unto God, who giveth us the victory.

Don't allow depression to be the end, allow God to remove it and give you a fresh start like He did for me.

Chapter 2

What Depression Has Done To Others

Depression is on the rise and there are millions around this world that battle with it on a daily basis. There are countless people I have known through the years that struggle with depression, and I'm sure you know many who do too. Depression is no game, and it's something that is literally taking over the world at a staggering rate. According to statistics, around 350 million people suffer from depression. I've heard many people describe to me how depression goes with them everywhere they go and they just can't seem to escape it. Many not only struggle with depression every year, but they ultimately lose the battle altogether. Statistics say that two-thirds of the 30,000 suicides that occur in the USA every year are caused from depression. The longer we stay in depression, the more dangerous it becomes. People come to me every day with stories about their depression that break my heart. They tell me that constantly throughout their day they cry, cut themselves, curl up in a corner, wish they were dead, and they don't even want to go on anymore. Depression is affecting my family, your family, my nation, and your nation, and it's important that we take this seriously.

When I announced I was writing this book, 100% of the people I told wanted one for themselves or a family member. This reality opened my eyes to the need of writing this book, and it revealed to me just how real this problem is. People are hurting like never before and depression is completely stopping millions in this world from living successful, productive lives. Every day dreams are never realized because of depression, and people are going out of their minds. Depression is causing people to be stressed, weighed down, and burdened with care. People by the untold thousands have stood up and admitted they need help with their depression and that they can't handle it alone. In these last days, the Devil is working overtime to keep people in depression. He knows his time is short and he will use every mental trick in his book to achieve it. Satan's goal is to depress as many as possible and to make them weak through the power of their mind. Many around this world are quitting, throwing in the towel, and allowing depression to rule their life. Depression is not going away and we must fight it off if we want to be a victor in life.

My prayer is that in the book to follow you will run to help when God points things out and get relief for your hurting soul. If we will not handle depression in our lives, we will never really enjoy life like we should and our journey will be an uphill climb. May God help us all to do what it takes to escape depression because it's hurting our country more and more, and if we continue to avoid this today we will only get worse, not better.

Chapter 3

What Depression Will Do To You

If you have never gone through the deep dark walls of depression, I praise God for that. But be aware that depression can sneak up like a thief in the night. No one is immune to depression, and it can strike anyone suddenly at any moment and it will not ask for permission to attack you. Once depression settles into your life, it can derail you and destroy you if not handled in a timely manner. Depression is nothing to mess around with and my advice would be to do whatever it takes to avoid it at all costs. If you are in your right mind, guard that because depression can take that from you. Depression literally has the potential of taking everything that you love and cherish and turn it into nothing but ashes. Depression in no way is your friend, and we better treat it as our enemy. Satan will use depression to make you feel sad, lonely, and broken. I've seen people that had it all end up on the streets begging and they were just a shell of their former self – all due to depression. I've seen countless singers, athletes, and artists end up on skid row begging for change all because depression took over their mind. Thousands of preachers who were once on fire for God have left the ministry and don't even attend church today all because of depression.

    Depression will make you crazy and like a tornado it will sweep over your soul and leave nothing but destruction in its wake. We must be aware of how dangerous depression can be, and we must understand that it can ruin our lives. Whenever we think it can't happen to us, most likely we will be the very person it attacks next. Please don't take depression into your bosom because it will burn you. Depression will take everything you have and want more so let's do whatever it takes to be in tune with God so it doesn't control our lives.

    In the chapters to come I pray you will see how important it is to gain victory over depression. If we take heed and run to these avenues for help, life will be sweeter and more enjoyable for all of us.

Chapter 4

When Depression Hits You, Run to Godly Music As Quick As You Can

The fastest way to overcome depression is to get saturated in the lyrics of good Godly music. Nothing on this earth can minister to the mind and inner-being more than Heaven-sent music can. The Bible teaches in I Samuel 16:23 that when Saul was struggling with an evil spirit his first option was to call in someone who was skilled in playing Godly music and when David played for him he was refreshed and his evil spirit departed. God has ordained music to bless, encourage, and strengthen hearts who are wounded from the battle. Godly music drives away doubt, confusion, hatred, and sorrow and replaces it with love, peace, serenity, and joy. God's music renews the mind, quickens the spirit, and sets you in Heavenly places mentally. I've seen preachers pay top dollar to bring in singers because any man of God understands what music can do for struggling people. When David felt defeated he surrounded himself with as many singers who lifted up God and it greatly encouraged him in the work of God. In Acts 16:25-26 the Bible says "And at midnight Paul and Silas prayed, and sang praises unto God: and the prisoners heard them. And suddenly there was a great earthquake, so that the foundations of the prison were shaken: and immediately all the doors were opened, and everyone's bands were loosed". If you are in a mental or spiritual prison singing praises to God can open the door to freedom in your life. Allow God's music to flow over your soul and drink it in like water on a hot summer day. Through the right kind of music God can change your attitude and make you new again. The Bible says in Colossians 3:16 "Let the Word of Christ dwell in you richly in all wisdom; teaching and admonishing one another in psalms and hymns and spiritual songs, singing with grace in your hearts to the Lord". Godly music can build you up, give you a boost, and refresh your mind. Ephesians 5:19 says "Speaking to yourselves in psalms and hymns and spiritual songs, singing and making melody in your hearts to the Lord". The Bible says to make a joyful noise unto the Lord. Whenever we sing unto the Lord depression will not be as bad and if we dwell on God's music enough depression will begin to go away.

The biggest mistake this world makes is when depression sweeps over them they run away from God's music and run towards Satan's music. The Devil's music will increase depression and rob us of every ounce of joy and victory we have. Satan's music preaches rebellion, hatred, violence, murder, pain, misery, sex, suicide, death, and eternal damnation. The Bible says that the Devil is the god of this world and he is blinding people to their need of Christ. Satan's following sadly is larger than Christ's following and because of this he is controlling the airwaves and the TV set and using it to destroy mankind's minds. Ever since rock and roll, rap, hip hop, and even country music came on the scene depression has grown at record numbers. Many of the so-called music stars of our day worship Satan and they are not shy about filling our youths minds with trash and filth. A famous preacher once said and I quote "I've never seen one person used of God that listens to Satan's music, it's impossible". The longer you allow Satan to fill your mind with garbage the more depression will invade your life. The Bible says if we resist the Devil he will flee from you. The Devil can only tempt you to do things but he cannot make us do anything.

Never underestimate the power of music both good and bad. Music has the power to lift your spirits to the throne room of God, or it has the ability to keep you locked up in the prison of your depression. If you are listening to Satan's music you are feeding a monster and your depression will grow to levels you never dreamed it could. Get rid of that junk right now and replace it with music that brings you comfort, victory, and triumph. Godly music can set you free from the torment of depression. The Bible says this in Isaiah 35:10 "And the ransomed of the Lord shall return, and come to Zion with songs and everlasting joy upon their heads: they shall obtain joy and gladness, and sorrow and sighing shall flee away". People come to me all the time crying and weeping because Satan has them bound in chains of depression. My advice to everyone in this position is to simply get rid of Satan's music and rejoice in God's music that can renew any mind and any spirit. The ones who listen gain help and the ones who don't get even worse. Don't allow Satan and his demons to control your mind any more - draw nigh to God and He will draw nigh to you. Flood your heart and mind with the right music and you will begin to break down the walls of depression and regain hope again.

CHAPTER 5

IF YOU WISH TO ESCAPE DEPRESSION, RUN AWAY FROM TEMPORAL THINGS, AND RUN TOWARDS ETERNAL THINGS

No matter what storm you find yourself in always remember that it's only temporal and it won't last forever. The great Apostle Paul said this in II Corinthians Ch 4:17 "For our light affliction which is but for a moment, worketh for us a far more exceeding and eternal weight of glory". The Bible says "Life is but a vapor" and the trails we encounter down here will be forever wiped away in glory. If the Devil can get you to focus on the nasty now and now he knows he can blind you to the brighter day that is coming. It's very hard to feel depressed when our mind is dwelling on Heaven, so Satan will come along and distract us through things of earth that will take our focus away from the eternal glory that awaits us. The Bible says "Love not the world, neither the things that are in the world.

If any man love the world the love of the Father is not in him. For all that is in the world, the lust of the flesh, and the lust of the eyes, and the pride of life, is not of the Father, but is of the world. And the world passeth away, and the lust thereof: but he that doeth the will of God abideth forever". When we dwell only on the temporal things it is a trap of the Devil and it will lead to depression every time. We must realize that Heaven and earth shall pass away but eternal things will remain forever. When we think about Heaven, depression must leave because the Bible says in Revelation 21:27 "And there shall in no wise enter into it anything that defileth, neither whatsoever worketh abomination, or maketh a lie: but they which are written in the lambs Book of Life". Focus on verses like John Ch 14:1-3 and depression will go away. The Bible says "Let not your heart be troubled: ye believe in God, believe also in me. In my Father's house are many mansions: if it were not so, I would have told you. I go to prepare a place for you. And if I go and prepare a place for you, I will come again. And receive you unto myself; that where I am, there ye may be also".

    Child of God, it's difficult to sense any depression when our minds are fixed on the joys that await us there. Revelation 21:4 says "And God shall wipe away all tears for their eyes: and there shall be no more death, neither sorrow, nor crying, neither shall there be any pain: for the former things are passed away". Heaven is a place of eternal bliss, joy, peace, freedom, and delight. In Heaven there will be no sickness, pain, fear, death, or depression. Thank God five seconds after we are in glory the pain we encountered on earth will be nothing more than a distant memory. The Bible says "For I reckon that the sufferings of this present time are not worthy to be compared with the glory, which shall be revealed in us". Nothing we face down here could ever compare to the glory we will enjoy up there. The Bible still says "O Death, where is thy sting? O grave, where is thy victory". Always keep your eyes on the ultimate prize and life will have meaning. The Bible says "Hence forth there is laid up for me a crown of righteousness, which the Lord, the Righteous Judge, shall give me at that day; and not to me only, but unto all them that love His appearing". The return of Christ is just over the horizon and if we can focus on that depression will fade in the background of our lives. The Bible says in Titus 2:13 "Looking for that blessed hope, and the glorious appearing of the great God and our Savior Jesus Christ". The scriptures declare in Revelation 22:12 "And behold, I come quickly; and my reward is with me, to give every man according as his work shall be". Will you have crowns to cast at His feet or are you too busy worrying about earthly things?

The Bible says in II Corinthians 5:10 "For we must all appear before the judgment seat of Christ; that every one may receive the things done in his body, according to that he hath done; whether it be good or bad". The Bible says that Christ shall return like a thief in the night. The Word of God says in I Corinthians 15:52 "In a moment, in the twinkling of an eye, Christ will return". Focusing on eternal things will thrust us out of depression and it will light a fire under us to be productive for God. Don't allow your life to be consumed with temporal things, allow God's Spirit to remind you of Heavenly things and depression will flee away from you. The Bible says set your affection on things above; and if we will have God's mind depression cannot be part of our daily routine. Don't allow Satan to keep you in the prison of your present, but rather allow your mind to be directed by the Holy Ghost and you will have a brand new outlook on life.

    Thank God for the saying "This too shall pass". Trials are but for a moment but Heaven will last throughout the ceaseless ages of eternity. Cheer up child of God and rest in the fact that God has a brighter day ahead for you.

Scriptures -- Chapter Five

II Corinthians 4:17: For a light affliction which is but for a moment, worketh in us a far more exceeding and eternal weight of glory.

Revelation 21:27: And there shall in no wise enter into it anything that defileth, neither whatsoever worketh abomination, or maketh a lie: but they which are written in the lambs Book of Life.

Revelation 21:4: And God shall wipe away all tears from their eyes: and there shall be no more death, neither shall there be any pain: for the former things are passed away.

Titus 2:13: Looking for that blessed hope, and the glorious appearing of the great God, and our Savior Jesus Christ.

Revelation 22:12 : And behold, I come quickly; and my reward is with me, to give to every man according as his work shall be.

Chapter 6

When You Feel Depressed, Help Others

There is something about helping others that pleases God and removes depression. The Bible says in Galatians 6:10 "As we have therefore opportunity, let us do good unto all men, especially unto them who are of the household of faith". The Bible says it is better to give than to receive. If you are busy doing good to others it takes your mind off your problems and makes you happy on the inside. The Lord said in Luke 6:38 "Give and it shall be given unto you, good measure, pressed down, and shaken together, and running over, shall men give unto your bosom". Jesus said in Matthew 20:28 "Even the son of man came not to be ministered unto, but to minister, and to give His life a ransom for many". Whenever a person spends his life building bigger barns for themselves God considers them a fool and depression will always revisit their lives time and time again. Whenever a person spends his life helping others you will see excitement, love and contentment. America is working themselves to death to get the newest boat, or the biggest house, and it results in stressed out people which leads to depression. The happiest people on earth are those who don't have much down here but have treasures up there. God wants us all to go the extra mile for other people, and die to our own selfish desires. Jude 22 says "of some have compassion making a difference". Focus your attention on helping others and depression will leave town. The Bible says "Set your affection on things above not on things on the earth". Jesus said "Lay not up for yourselves treasures upon earth, where moth and rust doth corrupt, and where thieves break through and steal. But lay up for yourselves treasures in Heaven, where neither moth nor rust doth corrupt, and where thieves do not break through nor steal". I've never met a giver who was an unhappy person, but I've met many greedy people who were mean as a snake. The key to living a God-honoring happy life is to spend your life helping others.

    Depression surrounds and torments those who refuse to help others. There is no greater feeling than being a blessing to others and those who do it often spend a very small percentage of their life in depression. Don't be a giver just around Christmas time, but rather make every day Christmas and help others in need. Depression always hovers over those who are self-centered and it always will. Make every day count, give on a daily basis and watch how the Lord fills you with benefits from above. God will shower down His blessings on anyone who helps others, and each blessing will be beyond human comprehension. The great Ronald Reagan once said "We can't help everyone, but everyone can help someone". All of us can be instrumental in impacting someone lives, and if we give we will impact ours as well. Another quote says "We rise by lifting others". People all around us need help and every time we reach out to help we in turn help ourselves as well. Giving brings joy, and joy does away with depression. A man once said "only a life lived for others, is a life worthwhile". Let's stop being selfish as Americans and let's start reaching the world and depression will not stick around.

The Word of God says in Philippians Ch 2:3 "Let nothing be done through strife or vain glory; but in lowliness of mind let each esteem others better than themselves". I John 3:16 says "Hereby perceive we the love of God: because He laid down His life for us: and we ought to lay down our lives for the brethren". Give your life for others and you will have less time thinking about yourself. Depression is basically a big pity party, but when you help others God's Spirit will crash that party and pull you out of there and make you useful again. Les Brown once said "Help others achieve their dreams and you will achieve yours". A great man once said "People who regularly help others are significantly happier and less likely to become depressed as they get older". If you start helping others today your tomorrow will be greater.

Let's end this chapter with a quote I love that says this "Helping other people can be a cure, not just for those who are in need, but for your soul as well". Determine to help others, and God will bring you out of the deep despairs of depression one soul at a time.

Scriptures -- Chapter Six

Galatians 6:10: As we have therefore opportunity, let us do good unto all men, especially unto them who are of the household of faith.

Luke 6:38: Give and it shall be given unto you, good measure, pressed down, and shaken together and running over, shall men give unto your bosom.

Matthew 20:28: Even the son of man came not to be ministered unto, but to minister, and give His life a ransom for many.

Jude 22: Of some have compassion making a difference.

Philippians 2:3: Let nothing be done through strife and vain glory; but in lowliness of mind let each esteem others better than themselves.

I John 3:16: Hereby perceive we the love of God: because He laid down His life for us: and we ought to lay down our lives for the brethren.

Chapter 7

When Depression Takes Over Pray, Pray, and Pray Some More

It is no secret to Christians that prayer is the answer for everything and it is key in getting rid of depression. When we are in constant fellowship with God, depression won't be present. The Word of God tells us to pray without ceasing and if we are right with God depression will not have a stronghold over our minds. Depression often sneaks up on us when we forsake our prayer closets and before too long we will have no power with God. Prayer is absent in so many lives and this leaves us open to Satan's attacks. If we desire for depression to leave us alone we must take the battle to higher ground through prayer. The Bible says in James 5:16 "That the effectual fervent prayer of a righteous man availeth much". Without a strong prayer life the Devil will gain advantages over us and we will not be effective for God. The Bible says in Jeremiah 33:3 "Call unto me, and I will answer thee, and show thee great and mighty things, which thou knowest not". In our day and age we don't even know what great things God can do because we never tap into His power. Years ago great men and women saw miracles, blessings, souls saved, lives transformed, and great and mighty things all because they knew how to get a hold of God. The Bible says in Psalm 55:16-17 "As for me, I will call upon God: and the Lord shall save me. Evening, and morning, and at noon, will I pray, and cry aloud: and He shall hear my voice". Psalm 34:6 says "This poor man cried, and the Lord heard him, and saved him out of all his troubles". If we are in depression we need to pray ourselves out of depression.

One of the greatest ways to fight off depression is through a consistent prayer life. The old saying says "The family who prays together stays together". When Satan gets us to stop talking to God, he then will whisper lies to us. The old quote says "Prayer is the link that connects us with God". Many great Christians in days gone by had a habit of praying for five hours a day and their power came from another world. Today, people may pray for five seconds and their minds are controlled by the underworld. People are too busy to pray so instead they miss out on God's power and they walk around defeated. Another quote says "If you only pray when you're in trouble...you're in trouble". There is a quote I love that says "Time spent in prayer is never wasted". Daniel Ch 6:10 says "Now when Daniel knew that the writing was signed, he went into his house; and his windows being open in his chamber toward Jerusalem, he kneeled upon his knees three times a day, and prayed, and gave thanks before his God, as he did aforetime". IF we don't pray we will fall and Satan will abuse us daily. Satan looks for the weak and when he finds them he has his way with them. When we are serious about prayer our attitudes will change and our boldness will stand out. Acts 4:31 says "And when they had prayed, the place was shaken where they were assembled together; and they were all filled with the Holy Ghost". Is prayer your steering wheel, or your spare tire? Do you allow prayer to direct your life, or do you just use it when you're in trouble?

The Bible says "But ye beloved, building up yourselves on your most holy faith, praying in the Holy Ghost". When Satan tries to take us down, we have the ability with God's help to build ourselves back up through prayer. One of my favorite quotes says this "Pray until your situation changes, miracles happen every day, so never stop believing, God can change things very quickly in your life". The Bible says in Matthew Ch 21:22 "And all things whatsoever ye shall ask in prayer, believing, ye shall receive". The Bible says "Ye have not because ye ask not". If you're in depression on a regular basis, let me ask you a question: When is the last time you got a prayer answered from God? IF it's been a long time, maybe that's the reason depression stays around. Prayer has the strength to force all depression away from us. A great quote says "No matter how alone you think you are God is always just a prayer away". We need to make prayer an active part of our lives and we can start going on the offensive instead of always being on the defensive. God desires to remove our fears and fill us with His power but without prayer it will never happen. The Bible says in Philippians 4:6 "Be careful for nothing, but in everything by prayer and supplication with thanksgiving let your requests be made unto God". The Lord is still on His throne working miracles and He will never go out of business. His power is limitless and His love for His people is infinite. It is up to us to approach Him in prayer; no one can do it for us. The

Bible says in Ephesians 6:18 "Praying always with all prayer and supplication in the spirit, and watching thereunto with all perseverance and supplication for all saints". To win against Satan we must pray it's that simple. Like with Job, God can build a hedge around us if we pray. If we don't, Satan will kick down the doors of our heart and mind and usher in depression. Someone once said and I quote "He who kneels before God can stand before anyone". Prayer is vital to the Christian life and if we cease to pray, prepare for a war every day. The great W. Clement Stone said "Prayer is a man's greatest power". Another great Christian said "Prayer is your personal key to Heaven". If prayer is so great, powerful, and effective, then why aren't we using it? I'll end with this quote and I hope you will pray away depression: "Prayer is the passport to spiritual power".

Scriptures -- Chapter Seven

James 5:16: The effectual fervent prayer of a righteous man avaleth much.

Jeremiah 33:3: Call unto me, and I will answer thee, and show thee great and mighty things, which thou knowest not.

Psalm 34:6: This poor man cried, and the Lord heard him, and saved him out of all his troubles.

Daniel 6:10: Now when Daniel knew that the writing was signed, he went into his house; and his windows being open in his chamber toward Jerusalem, he kneeled upon his knees three time a day, and prayed, and gave thanks before his God, and he did aforetime.

Acts 4:31: And when they had prayed, the place was shaken where they were assembled together; and they were all filled with the Holy Ghost.

Ephesians 6:18: Praying always with all prayer and supplication in the spirit, and watching thereunto with all perseverance

Chapter 8

In Order to Get Out of Depression, We Must Leave the Darkness and Step into the Light

Depravity and darkness fills our nature from head to toe and in order to slay depression we must leave the darkness and step into the light. The Bible says "Men loved darkness rather than light, because their deeds are evil". Without Christ, we are dark, evil, wicked, and destined for trouble. The Bible says in Proverbs 4:19 "The way of the wicked is as darkness: they know not at what they stumble". When you join hands with Satan, depression will always be close by. The Bible says in Job 12:25 "They grope in the dark without light, and he maketh them to stagger like a drunken man". The Bible says in Matthew 6:23 "But if thine eye be evil, thy whole body shall be full of darkness. If therefore the light that is in thee be darkness, how great is that darkness". If you are content dwelling in the darkness no one can help you. Feeding your flesh with darkness will play into Satan's hands and you will bite off more than you can chew and the Devil will destroy you. If you play around with darkness, you will be a loser every time and Satan will control your every action. In order to escape depression we must make a conscious decision to leave the darkness and come into the light.

The only way we will ever be happy is if we leave the world, flesh, and the Devil behind and walk into the glorious light of the Gospel of Jesus Christ. The Bible says in Ephesians 5:14 "Wherefore he saith, awake thou that sleepest, and arise from the dead, and Christ shall give thee light". Romans 13:12 says "The night is far spent, the day is at hand; let us therefore cast off the works of darkness, and let us put on the armor of light". In these last days so many are sleep walking and without light they will stagger into the pit of Hell. The only hope we have to get out of depression is to surround ourselves with as much light as possible. Jesus said in John 8:12 "I am the light of the world: he that followeth me shall not walk in darkness but shall have the light of life". Proverbs 4:18 says "But the path of the just is as a shining light that shineth more and more unto the perfect day". The more light you surround yourself with the more darkness will go away. Light and darkness cannot dwell with one another and the key to destroying depression altogether is to bask in the sunlight of God's love. I John 1:5 says "This then is the message which we have heard of Him, and declare unto you, that God is light, and in Him is no darkness at all". Feed your spirit far more than you feed your flesh and the light will win over the darkness. Revelation 21:23 says "And the city had no need of the sun, neither of the moon, to shine in it; for the glory of God did lighten it, and the lamb is the light thereof". Jesus has enough light to dispel any darkness and one day He will destroy death by the brightness of His coming. Until then, we must defeat the powers of darkness through the light of the Lord, Jesus Christ, and shine bright to everyone around us. Run from darkness and depression will run from you. I John 1:7 says "But walk in the light as He is in the light, we have fellowship one with another, and the blood of Jesus Christ His son cleanseth us from all sin". Depression will run from all those who walk in the light.

Scriptures -- Chapter Eight

John 3:19: And this is the condemnation, that light is come into the world, and men loved darkness rather than light, because their deeds were evil.

Proverbs 4:19: The way of the wicked is as darkness: they know not at what they stumble.

Job 12:25: They grope in the dark without light, and he maketh them to stagger like a drunken man.

Matthew 6:23: But if thine eye be evil, thy whole body shall be full of darkness. If therefore the light that is in thee be darkness, how great is that darkness.

Ephesians 5:14: Wherefore he saith, awake thou that sleepest, and arise from the dead, and Christ shall give thee light.

Romans 13:12: The night is far spent, the day is at hand; let us therefore cast off the works of darkness, and let us put on the armor of light.

John 8:12: Then spoke Jesus again unto them, saying, I am the light of the world: he that followeth me shall not walk in darkness but shall have the light of life.

Proverbs 4:18: But the path of the just is as a shining light that shineth more and more unto the perfect day.

I John 1:5: This then is the message which we have heard

of Him, and declare unto you, that God is light, and in Him is no darkness at all.

Revelation 21:23: And the city had no need of the sun, neither the moon, to shine in it; for the glory of God did lighten it, and the lamb is the light thereof.

Chapter 9

If You Feel Like You Can't Escape Depression, Run to Praise and Worship

If you are going through a deep dark valley do yourself a favor and worship God with everything inside you. The Devil hates when God's children worship the Lord in Spirit and in truth, and when you praise God the Devil won't be able to handle that too long. God has designed mankind to praise and worship Him and to have fellowship with Him in the cool of the day. Shouting and praising God drives depression away and it can turn your sadness into glory very quickly. David donated hundreds of verses to the subject of worship and if you really want to make Satan mad worship the Lord despite how you feel. Psalm 150:6 says "Let everything that hath breath praise the Lord, praise ye he Lord". There have been many times over the years that I've praised God through may pain and before the night was over I couldn't even remember what was bothering me. Praising the Lord will remove all fear and if we could just unplug from our problems and get plugged into worship depression will be a thing of the past.

In our churches today people come in with their lips dragging the ground and their refusal to worship kills the Spirit in God's house. The Bible still says where the Spirit of the Lord is, there is liberty. Without worship depression will linger and liberty with God will be missing. The song "Brethren We Have Met to Worship" should be changed to "Brother We Have Met to Grieve the Spirit, Backbite, and Gossip" because people know nothing about biblical worship and Satan loves it. I've gone into some churches that were so cold and bitter that during the music I could not even move my lips because the spirit was so dead. God wants His services alive, vibrant, and full of praise because He has ordained for us to worship in Spirit and in truth. Whenever I shout for God and worship people look at me like I'm nuts and an alien from another planet. Worship is missing in our lives and churches and it results in defeated lives. There is nothing like feeling His power on the inside and letting it out for the world to hear. It's strange to me that people have no problem paying hundreds of dollars to shout at a ball game but come into church and sit there like a bump on a log. If we get more excited over a game than we do church we need to ask God to forgive us. Depression is like a magnet to those who doubt instead of shout. Paul said this in Philippians 4:4 "Rejoice in the Lord always: and again I say, rejoice". When the Devil takes your shout he will soon knock you out. The next time you feel the shackles of depression weighing you down throw both hands in the air and worship.

Many who came to Jesus felt hopeless and before they asked for anything they worshipped and this attitude brought a healing from God. God wants us to worship at all times because He is ever faithful. Christians need to learn how important worship is when it comes to defeating depression. The God of the mountain is still God in the valley. Worthy is the lamb who was slain. The Bible says "Great is the Lord, and greatly to be praised and His greatness is unsearchable". Focus on God's greatness instead of your fears and any storm of doubt and depression can disappear. The Bible says "Let the high praises of God be in their mouth, and a two-edged sword in their hand". Praising and worshipping God will please the Lord and cause Satan to run from you. Depression is no match for those who praise Him. Give it a try and see what happens. You cannot worship and be sad at the same time. The next time the Devil comes around shout so loud that he needs earplugs and your depression will start to fade away.

Scriptures -- Chapter Nine

Psalm 150:6: Let everything that hath breath praise the Lord, praise ye the Lord.

Philippians 4:4: Rejoice in the Lord always: and again I say, rejoice.

Psalm 149:6: Let the high praises of God be in their mouth, and a two-edged sword in their hand.

Psalm 147:5: Great is the Lord, and of great power: His understanding is infinite.

Chapter 10

When Depression is Near, Run to God's House

The Bible says this in Matthew 16:18 "And I say also unto thee that thou art Peter, and upon this rock I will build my church and the gates of Hell shall not prevail against it". When you are going through depression, the worst thing for you is to be alone and the best thing for you is to be in a church where the gates of Hell cannot get in. In God's house you can find rest, love, mercy, guidance, charity, faith, peace, and relief. The Bible says in Psalm 92:13 "Those that be planted in the house of the Lord shall flourish in the courts of our God". When you are faithful to God's house you will flourish and depression will be conquered. David said "Surely goodness and mercy shall follow me all the days of my life: and I will dwell in the house of the Lord forever". Always remember it only takes one service, one move of God, or one breath from above, and your depression can be taken care of. The Bible says in Psalm 27:4 "One thing have I desired of the Lord, that will I seek after; that I may dwell in the house of the Lord all the days of my life; to behold the beauty of the Lord, and to inquire in His temple". The Devil wants you to stay in your house and cry when depression hits you but God wants you in His house so His Spirit can deliver you. In these last days depression is at an all-time high and people are making the mistake of missing God's house. The Bible says in Hebrews 10:25 "Not forsaking the assembling of ourselves together as the manner of some is; but exhorting one another; and so much the more, as you see the day approaching". The more we forsake God's house the more depression will haunt us. Inside the church walls there is protection, favor, songs of joy, preaching, saints who care, God's Spirit, love, friends, family, and an altar to pray at.

When you are in depression sometimes it's just hard to make it to God's house but you must determine to make it no matter what it takes. God's house is the house of bread, the house of prayer, and the house of miracles and if you can make it great things are bound to happen. Years ago I watched a man with Parkinson's disease walk across the church parking shaking like a leaf and struggling to take each step. Every move he made looked painful but as he made it inside the church his shaking would stop and his relief would come. He told me that the biggest struggle for him would just be to make it but he knew if he could God would take care of the rest. This dear brother would get up, play the piano, and sing with perfect control and anointing. There is power within the walls of God's house and if you can just get there miracles can and will happen. Psalm 122:1 says "I was glad when they said unto me, let us go into the house of the Lord". The Bible says in Psalm 84:10 "For a day in thy courts is better than a thousand. I had rather be a doorkeeper in the house of my God, than to dwell in the tents of the wickedness". When we are faithful to God's house you will thrive and your chances of remaining in deep depression will drop substantially. Life is a rollercoaster of highs and lows but the constant theme of our life should be extreme faithfulness to God's house. Don't let any emotion, hardship, or sudden fear take you from God's house. If Satan can keep us out of church, he can flood our minds with lies, deception, and depression much easier than he could if we were in God's house. God's house will provide shelter from the enemy, food for the soul, and water for the spirit. Run to God's house every chance you get, resist the Devil and he will flee from you.

Scriptures -- Chapter Ten

Matthew 16:18: And I say also unto thee that thou art Peter, and upon this rock I will build my church and the gates of Hell shall not prevail against it.

Psalm 92:13: Those that be planted in the house of the Lord shall flourish in the courts of our God.

Psalm 23:6: Surely goodness and mercy shall follow me all the days of my life: and I shall dwell in the house of the Lord forever.

Psalm 27:4: One thing have I desired of the Lord, that will I seek after; that I may dwell in the house of the Lord all the days of my life; to behold the beauty of the Lord, and to inquire in His temple.

Hebrews 10:25: Not forsaking the assembling of ourselves together as the manner of some is; but exhorting one another; and so much the more, as you see the day approaching.

Psalm 122:1: I was glad when they said unto me, let us go into the house of the Lord.

Psalm 84:10: For a day in thy courts is better than a thousand. I had rather be a doorkeeper in the house of my God, than to dwell in the tents of wickedness.

Chapter 11

When You're Battling Depression, Run Towards Positive Thinking

The Word of God teaches us that we come forth speaking lies and that we are full of trouble. There is something about fallen man that has a tendency to forget the good and remember the bad. David said in sin did my mother conceive me, and the old song writer wrote "Prone to Wonder Lord I Feel It, Prone to Leave the God I Love". There is something about our wicked nature that pulls us away from a positive mindset but if we want to get out of depression we must train our minds to be positive. The Bible says in Isaiah 26:3 "Thou wilt keep him in perfect peace, whose mind is stayed on thee: because he trusteth in thee". The Apostle Paul talked much about staying positive no matter what happens to us throughout life. Paul knew the dangers of being negative and the powers of being positive and over and over again he tried to encourage people to think positive. In Romans Ch 8:6 the great Apostle Paul wrote this "For to be carnally minded is death; but to be spiritually minded is life and peace". When a person constantly dwells on negativity it won't be long before depression will show up on at the front door. Positive holy thinking can drive depression away and it can bring life and peace in our lives. The Bible says in Philippians 4:8 "Finally, brethren, whatsoever things are honest, whatsoever things are just, whatsoever things are pure, whatsoever things are lovely, whatsoever things are of a good report, if there be any praise, think on these things". Our nation and our churches should be filled with people on fire, excited, zealous and ready to charge Hell with a squirt gun but sadly people fill our pews broken, sad, defeated, and quiet. God's people should be the happiest people on earth but the majority of Christians are cold, bitter, and miserable. Every time we turn on the TV or read the newspaper in these last days all we see is doom and gloom. The Devil is pumping our brains with negativity and revival is a thousand miles from us. We should wake up every morning with a *tackle the world* attitude and a conquering spirit. The Bible still says "As a man thinketh in his heart, so is he". If we are positive we will accomplish greatness, but if we are negative we will always feel defeated. A great motivational speaker once said this statement and I quote "Statistics reveal that around 83% of what people do or think is negative".

When a person chooses to be negative depression will tend to hang over them like a dark cloud. When we are positive we will expect great things and depression will flee away from our lives. The Bible says in Job 1:21 "Naked came I out of my mother's womb, and naked shall I return thither: the Lord gave, and the Lord taketh away, blessed be the name of the Lord". We must train our minds to remain positive no matter what happens and depression will vanish away. The old song writer said this "Count your many blessings, name them one by one and it will surprise you what the Lord hath done". David said "This is the day that the Lord hath made, let us be glad and rejoice in it". Life is too short to be miserable all the time, renew your mind in the goodness of God and watch how much it helps you. God wants us to fly for His glory and being positive will provide the wings to do just that. Romans 8:28 says "And we know that all things work together for good to them that love God, to them who are the called according to His purpose". Every single one of us has a purpose for living and I promise that purpose does not involve being tormented through depression. Spend your life thinking positive and you will enjoy life more and you will spend far less time being sad. Jesus said in John 16:33 "In this world ye shall have tribulation but be of good cheer I have overcome the world". We can overcome depression and through God's Spirit we can live in victory every day. Child of God, take a deep breath, hold your head up high, and have confidence that God will help you every step of the way and your sadness will be turned into gladness.

Scriptures -- Chapter Eleven

Romans 8:6: For to be carnally minded is death; but to be spiritually minded is life and peace.

Philippians 4:8: Finally, brethren, whatsoever things are honest, whatsoever things are pure, whatsoever things are lovely, whatsoever things are of a good report, if there be any praise, think on these things.

Job 1:21: Naked came I out of my mother's womb, and naked shall I return thither: the Lord gave, the Lord taketh away, blessed be the name of the Lord.

John 16:33: In this world ye shall have tribulation but be of good cheer I have overcome the world.

Chapter 12

If You Are in Depression, Run Towards Joy Whatever the Cost

If the Devil can manage to steal our joy he knows he will be successful in taking our strength and depressing our emotions. The Bible is clear in Nehemiah 8:10 that the joy of the Lord is our strength and if he can steal our strength he will devour us because he is a roaring lion. Without joy flowing in our lives Satan will discourage us, he will derail us, and he will destroy us. The Bible teaches that we are to put on the fruit of the Spirit and the whole armor of God. When David lost his joy, he was not the same and he begged God for it again. David knew he was weak, frail, and defeated without his joy and his number one goal was to get it back as fast as he could. When we lack joy, Satan will have a field day in our lives. The Devil laughs at us when our joy is gone and without strength we are no match against his fiery darts. Misery loves company and when he gets people suicidal he delights in it. God wants to fill you with His joy and if you will seek hard after it He will free you from Satan's strong grip. The Bible says in Psalm 16:11 "Thou wilt show me the path of life: in thy presence is fullness of joy: at thy right hand there are pleasures ever more". The Bible says in Jude 24 "Now unto Him that is able to keep you from falling, and to present you faultless before the presence of His glory with exceeding great joy". God intends for all mankind to walk with joy unspeakable and full of glory free from depression, hardship, and fear. People all over this world just roll over and allow Satan to beat them down and they live in His dungeon on a daily basis.

We as Christians need to realize how important our joy is and fight Satan tooth and nail through the power of God's Spirit. Depression cannot stay when joy is around; they do not coexist. If you want your life and mind back it's a must that you get your joy back. Far too many people have lost their joy and it's made them miss out on so much God had planned for them. Refuse to forfeit any more of your future blessings for God. Get up, leave the Devil where he stands, and search for joy with all the strength you presently have. The Bible says in Isaiah 40:29 "He giveth power to the faint: and to them that have no might He increaseth strength". No matter how weak and alone you feel always remember there is a friend that sticketh closer than a brother and He can make you strong again. Satan desires to keep you weak but God who is greater is able to make you strong. If you make a step towards God, He will make a step towards you. No matter how low you feel, one touch from the Master can drive depression far away. The Bible says "Greater is He that is in me, than he that is in the world". If you make your way towards God, He will restore your joy and your life and Satan will be the one who leaves defeated. Isaiah 40:31 says "But they that wait upon the Lord shall renew their strength; they shall mount up with wings as eagles: they shall run and not be weary; and they shall walk and not faint". We can either soar for God through this avenue of joy, or lay around in depression without strength and without a reason to live. Don't fall prey to Satan's lies anymore; get joy in your life and everything will make sense again.

    We can fully escape depression when we discover joy in the Lord.

Scriptures -- Chapter Twelve

Nehemiah 8:10: The joy of the Lord is your strength.

Jude 24: Now unto Him that is able to keep you from falling, and to present you faultless before the presence of His glory with exceeding great joy.

Psalm 16:11: Thou wilt show me the path of life: in thy presence is fullness of joy: at thy right hand there are pleasures ever more.

Isaiah 40:29: He giveth power to the faint: and to them that have no might He increaseth strength.

Isaiah 40:31: But they that wait upon the Lord shall renew their strength; they shall mount up with wings as eagles: they run and not be weary; and they shall walk and not faint.

I John 4:4: Greater is He that is in me, than he that is in the world.

Chapter 13

When Depression Strikes, It's Wise to Run to God's Throne

It amazes me what people run to when the deep walls of depression close in around them. People's first reaction is to run to drugs, drinking, parties, fun, and other avenues, but little do they know that those choices are hurting them and causing them to sink deeper in despair. In America, people choose to run towards everything that won't work and as a last resort turn to God. As depression rises church attendance drops and we wonder why people are in trouble. Millions around this world are struggling and if they would just run to God's Throne their depression would turn into peace and they could get the answers they seek. God has not gone out of business and His vast power and ability to heal will never run out. When stress rises in your life, stop running to shrinks, doctors, or man's methods, but rather take it to a higher source. All the answers you seek can be found at the Throne Room of Grace and if you will go to His Throne you can walk away healed and delivered from depression. The Bible makes this promise to any child of God in Hebrews 4:16. Here is what this powerful verse says "Let us therefore come boldly unto the Throne of Grace, that we may obtain mercy, and grace to help in time of need". When we need mercy we can find it at the Throne. If we need grace we can find it at the Throne. If we need help we can find it at the Throne along with every other answer we need that bothers us. Take your burdens to the Lord and leave them there.

So many try so many different things to deal with their struggles and at the end of trying they find themselves in a deeper hole than when they started. Jesus has every answer you need and when you go to His Throne for help He will come through each and every time. David said this in Psalm 61:1-1 "hear my cry, O God; attend unto my prayer. From the end of the earth will I cry unto thee, when my heart is overwhelmed, lead me to the rock that is higher than I". David knew when troubles came and his heart was overwhelmed that the greatest way to gain help was to run towards God's Throne. Many in this day and age add to their problems by overthinking and trying to figure out how to deal with their problems while all the time God has made it very simple. If we could learn that God's Throne is the solution to any problem we face we could live a happier, more carefree, life. Psalm 46:10 says "Be still and know that I am God".

During depression, the Devil wants to speed up your mind and cause you to worry about your problems. The Bible, however, teaches that when depression comes we need to slow down and rest in the fact that God is the answer and He will be our present help in time of trouble. The Devil trains minds that no one cares about us and we would be better off not existing at all. The Bible says in I Peter 5:7 "Casting all your care upon Him, *speaking of God) for He careth for you". The Devil will make you feel worthless when you go through depression and you will feel like there is no way out. Let me just say that God loves you and that is a lie straight from Hell because there is always a way out. Psalm 40:17 says "But I am poor and needy; yet the Lord thinketh upon me: thou art my help and my deliverer; make no tarrying, O My God".

    The New Testament always says God loves you and He is praying for you. The Bible declares that God is love and in Him there is no darkness at all. The Bible teaches us time and time again that God loves us and He gave His life for us. Do not believe the Devil's lies because he is the father of lies. Trust that God cares for you and swiftly run to His Throne for help when depression brings you down. Always remember when you are going through depression that Satan will cause your mind to worry and race and you will feel like you can't get a grip on your thoughts or slow them down. Satan's plan is to toy with your mind and make you think too fast so you cannot enjoy life. God always wants you to slow down, look above, and trust Him through your storms. Never allow your mind to feel like it's in a race because you will never have peace that way. Be patient, rest in God's love, and run to His Throne when depression invades your life. Run to God's Throne and you will find the answers. There is hope, mercy, help, and triumph at His Throne. Nothing down here will be as effective to the power you feel up there. Make life simple; make God's Throne your first option and watch your life come back together. God's arms are open and He is willing and able to help you with any problem you have. The Bible says in John 6:37 "All that the

Father giveth me shall come to me: and Him that cometh to me I will in no wise cast out". If you're in a mess go to Jesus for rest and He will satisfy your every need. Jesus loves you, and cherishes you. Don't waste another moment, flee to His Throne for He is the solution to your depression. The Bible says in Matthew 11:28 "Come unto me all ye, that labor and are heavy laden, and I will give you rest". Stop running to the Devil's avenues and run to the only avenue that can really help you and that is at the feet of Jesus. He will forgive you, restore your mind, and bring you out of depression but you must answer the call and come today. Many reading this chapter desperately need rest and it won't be found in anything but Christ. Thank God for the Throne of Grace for it has the ability to restore any in need.

Scriptures -- Chapter Thirteen

Hebrews 4:16: Let us therefore come boldly unto the Throne of Grace, that we may obtain mercy, and grace to help in time of need.

Psalm 61:12: Hear my cry, O God; attend unto my prayer. From the end of the earth will I cry unto thee, when my heart is overwhelmed, lead me to the rock that is higher than I.

Psalm 46:10: Be still and know that I am God.

I Peter 5:7: Casting all your care upon Him, for He careth for you.

Psalm 40:17: But I am poor and needy; yet the Lord thinketh upon me: thou art my helper and my deliverer; make no tarrying, O My God.

John 6:37: All that the Father giveth me shall come to me: and Him that cometh to me I will in no wise cast out.

Matthew 11:28: Come unto me all ye, that labor and are heavy laden, and I will give you rest.

Chapter 14

Run to the Prince of Peace When You Can't Get a Handle on Depression

All types of depression are different but when I read Mark Ch. 5 it gives me the sense that there is hope for any type of depression if people would just do what the crazy man did and run to the Prince of Peace. In Mark Ch. 5 we read about a man who tried everything but nothing seemed to work and night and day he cried and cut himself with stones. The Bible teaches that this maniac ran around naked and he was seemly beyond help and beyond hope. One day after exhausting all strength he looked through the storm and seen a man who calmed the stormy weather with just three words: Peace Be Still; and immediately there was a great calm and all his fears melted away. When Jesus came to shore this crazy man ran to Jesus and from that day forward he was never the same again. The Bible says that this crazy man was seated, and clothed, and in his right mind and every one of his 6000 demons were cast out by the power of God. Immediately a great change came in this man's life and it didn't take weeks or years to happen but it was instant. When we finally run to the Prince of Peace with the desire for help a great change can take place. The Bible in II Corinthians 5:17 says "Therefore if any man be in Christ, he is a new creature; old things are passed away: behold all things are become new". No matter how many demons you possess or how many fears fill your heart they can all be removed if you will just run to Jesus.

The Bible teaches that perfect love casteth out fear, and when Jesus moves in Satan must move out. The Bible says God hath not given us the spirit of fear and with God controlling our life depression can be overcome. The Bible says in Jeremiah 29:13 "And ye shall seek me, and find me, when ye shall search for me with all your heart". If you turn your life, mind, and soul over to God fully fear will go away and peace will fill your heart. When the maniac finally got tired of his condition he ran to Jesus because he knew Jesus was the only hope he had. If Jesus can give a man like this peace he can give you peace as well. The Bible says in Isaiah 9:6 "For unto us a child is born, unto us a son is given: and the government shall be upon His shoulder: and His name shall be called wonderful, counselor, the Mighty God, the Everlasting Father, the Prince of Peace". Let me ask you this question: if Jesus is the only one who can give you peace then why do we refuse Him and accept everything else? The Devil can give you pleasure, fun, and excitement but it's impossible for him to offer peace. Jesus wants to give us peace but instead most will shun his help and ruin their lives through foolish, stupid, choices. The Bible says in Philippians 4:7 "And the peace of God, which passeth all understanding, shall keep your hearts and minds through Christ Jesus". Jesus can clean any drunk up through His blood and give them peace. Jesus can cure any disease, mental affliction, drug addict, or sin through

His blood and peace will enter in. The story of the crazy man can give anyone hope because he went through depression for the majority of his life and in a seconds time Jesus took care of all of it.

When Jesus passes by your way don't be a fool. Reach out and grab the hem of His garment and He can free your mind and heal your wounded spirit. Never give up on life or lose your hope for life because that's what Satan desires. Believe that the sun will shine again for you through the power that is in Jesus Christ. Psalm 40:1-3 says "I waited patiently for the Lord: and He inclined unto me, and heard my cry. He brought me up also out of a horrible pit, out of the miry clay, and set my feet upon a rock, and established my goings. And He hath put a new song in my mouth, even praise unto our God: many shall see it, and fear, and shall trust in the Lord". It does not matter what kind of a pit you find yourself in, Jesus has the strength and ability to pull you out and place you upon a rock. If you feel like you're in chains of bondage, fear, and torment, Jesus, the Prince of Peace, can break every chain. Psalm 68:6 says "God setteth the solitary in families: He bringeth out those which are bound with chains: but the rebellious dwell in a dry land". There is hope for the broken, and deliverance through Jesus.

I've seen many through the years who have been delivered from depression and the same is true with all of these cases. They all will admit that without Jesus touching them and breaking their chains they would still be weak, frail, and in bondage. Keep life very simple, swallow your pride, and run to Jesus and you will be a happy camper. Far too many add sorrow upon sorrow and the Devil keeps them all tied up and miserable.

If Jesus offers peace and Satan offers fear why would anyone choose Satan's way over Gods? Make up your mind to run to Jesus and He can transform your mind, heart, life, and future. Mark Ch. 5:15 says this "And they came to Jesus, and see him that was possessed with the Devil, and had the legion, sitted, and clothed, and in his right mind: and they were afraid". Go to Jesus for the peace you desire and your tears will be tears of joy not tears of pain. If God can heal the maniac and set him on a new path He can do the same for you. Allow Jesus to free you from the prison of your fear and let Him use you for His honor and glory. Always remember this quote "When hope is all gone, help is on the way". A great man once said "Don't give up, don't ever give up". There is hope in Christ and if you reach out in desperation He will respond to your cry for help and deliver you as only He can.

Scriptures -- Chapter Fourteen

II Corinthians 5:17: Therefore if any man be in Christ, he is a new creature; old things are passed away: behold all things are become new.

Jeremiah 29:13: And ye shall seek me, and find me, when ye shall search for me with all your heart.

Isaiah 9:6: For unto us a child is born, unto us a son is given: and the government shall be upon His shoulder: and His name shall be called wonderful, counsellor, the Might God, the Everlasting Father, the Prince of Peace.

Philippians 4:7: And the peace of God, which passeth all understanding, shall keep your hearts and minds through Christ Jesus.

Psalm 68:6: God setteth the solitary in families; He bringeth out those which are bound with chains: but the rebellious dwell in a dry land.

Mark 5:15: And they came to Jesus, and see him that was possessed with the Devil, and had the legion, sitted, and clothed, and in his right mind: and they were afraid.

Chapter 15

Run Towards a Forgiving Spirit and You Can Get Out of Depression

The Word of God teaches how dangerous it is to hold bitterness towards others and how fatal it is to have unforgiveness in our hearts. Bitterness and unforgiveness will absolutely kill the fruit of the Spirit in our lives and it has the ability to throw anyone of us into a deep depression. The Bible says in Ephesians 4:32 "Be ye kind one to another, tenderhearted, forgiving one another, even as God for Christ's sake hath forgiven you". Jesus told Peter to forgive people 490 times a day, and there are people all over this world who were wronged 40 years ago and they still won't forgive that person. The Bibles says "Let not the sun go down upon your wrath" or in other words: don't carry unforgiveness to bed with you. I've literally watched bitterness eat people up from the inside out spiritually and it has taken their love, joy, and blessings from them. Millions around this world could get relief from depression if they would just forgive those who have hurt them. Personally I could take you to so many Christian's who once were on fire from God, but now they lay around depressed all because of an unforgiving spirit. All of us have been hurt. But all of us have the power to forgive. Hatred, anger, and strife fill the hearts of millions around this world and forgiveness could instantly take care of all of it and depression could drop dramatically.

    Unforgiveness and bitterness are the greatest tools Satan is using to knock people out of the will of God. When Saul got jealous, angry, and bitter towards David that was the beginning of the end for King Saul. Once Saul developed these tendencies towards David God gave him an evil spirit and he was never the same again. Bitterness and unforgiveness have the potential to cause great damage to our emotions, spirit, soul, and mind, and if we harbor these two sins we are asking for trouble. God wants us to walk in love and if we do depression will not control our lives. If someone has wronged you, forgive them, and you can go from depression to joy in a matter of seconds. When Jesus was hanging on the cross He said "Father, forgive them for they know not what they do". If Jesus could do it while suffering the worst death ever known to man then we can as well. Have a forgiving spirit all your days and you will feel depression disappearing from your life.

    Go to people who have hurt you, forgive them, and I promise you will walk away a whole new person by the grace of God.

Scriptures -- Chapter Fifteen

Ephesians 4:32: Be ye kind one to another, tenderhearted, forgiving one another, even as God for Christ's sake hath forgiven you.

Ephesians 4:26: Be ye angry, and sin not: let not the sun go down upon your wrath.

Chapter 16

When You Are Depressed, Run to the History Books for Help

One thing that has helped me beyond measure to deal with depression is studying history of those who have had a much tougher road than I have. History is filled with people who went through the fire, spiritually speaking, and came out on the other side as pure gold. Isaiah Ch. 43:2 says "When thou passeth through the waters, I will be with thee: and through the rivers, they shall not overflow thee: when thou walkest through the fire, thou shalt not be burned: neither shall the flame kindle upon thee".

Many of the great hymns were born out of great affliction and trials that people went through. Many of the song writers suffered loss of health, loss of children, loss of land, loss of families, but nothing stopped them from doing God's work. Mrs. Fanny Crosby was blind, had a bad marriage, lost a child, had many hard times, but she maintained her joy, and wrote around 9000 hymns. Mrs. Nancy Dodrige lost 19 kids to death but she refused to give up and later raised her 20th child who went on to write the song "O Happy Day" that helped millions. Some of the greatest preachers suffered deep valleys of depression and the loss of many things but they accomplished greatness despite their obstacles. Mr. Charles Spurgeon was known to spend months in depression due largely to the amount of pressure he was under but he pushed through it and accomplished more spiritually than anyone of his time. If I had the time I could list hundreds, if not thousands, of people who were dealt a horrible hand in life but used their depression as fuel for greatness.

    We can handle depression in two different ways. We can either use it to make us bitter, or we can use it to make us stronger. Thousands upon thousands of people have allowed depression to destroy them, and that is certainly what Satan wants. On the other hand, untold thousands, even millions, have used their dark times of depression as a teaching aid and a learning tool to help others. Paul said "I will glory in my infirmities, that the power of Christ may rest upon me". Job said "Though He slay me yet will I trust in Him". If you will take whatever depresses you and give it over to God, He can make you stronger for His work. The Devil loves to convince folks that they are alone, and no one else has gone through what they are going through, and he will hammer this home in people's minds when they are depressed. History along with God's Word proves this to be a lie and it's simply not the truth. According to God's Word, everyone has struggles, but it's how we handle it that will determine if we will shine for God. The Bible says it rains on the just and on the unjust. The Word of God says "Many are the afflictions of the righteous; but the

Lord delivereth him out of them all". The Bible says that "Man is born of a woman is of few days, and full of trouble".

Don't allow Satan to get you in a dark corner somewhere and torture your mind with the lie that no one understands. All around this world people suffer and you are not alone. Use your depression to make you stronger and use it to help others. Jesus told Peter "When thou art converted strengthen thy brethren". The Bible says in Job 23:10 "But He knoweth the way I take: when He hath tried me, I shall come forth as gold". No matter how alone you feel, God has a plan for your life and the Bible teaches us that the trial of our faith worketh patience. The Bible says in Proverbs 3:5-6 "Trust in the Lord with all thine heart; and lean not unto thine own understanding. In all thine ways acknowledge Him, and He shall direct thy paths". Always remember all storms must end, and God has a purpose for everything He does. Trust God's Word over your emotions and you will come out on the other side as a precious jewel. All around us are people going through battles and we are not alone. Don't allow Satan to make you feel hopeless. Study history, realize many have gone through far worse, and rejoice in all the blessings you do have and your depression will not be as bad. Romans 8:28 says "And we know that all things work together for good to them that love God, to them who are the called according to His purpose". Remind yourself you have purpose and if you refuse to throw in the towel God can use you in a great and special way.

Every time I find myself in a storm of depression I slow down, pace myself, and focus on how good God has been, and how much worse it could be. You do not have to read too deep into history or look too far around to discover that compared to other's situations ours is not that bad after all. Praise God through your depression, and thank Him for all the good things you do have. Psalm 33:5 says "The earth is full of the goodness of the Lord". Focus on your blessings, not your problems and understand that it could be a whole lot worse. There is so much to be thankful for.

Scriptures -- Chapter Sixteen

Isaiah 43:2: When thou passeth through the waters, I will be with thee: and through the rivers, they shall not overflow thee: when thou walkest through the fire, thou shalt not be burned: neither shall the flame kindle upon thee.

II Corinthians 12:9: And he said unto me, my grace is sufficient for thee: for my strength is made perfect in weakness. Most gladly therefore will I rather glory in my infirmities, that the power of Christ may rest upon me.

Job 13:15: Though He slay me, yet will I trust in Him: but I maintain mine own ways before Him.

Psalm 34:19: Many are the afflictions of the righteous: but the Lord delivereth him out of them all.

Job 14:1: Man that is born of a woman is of few days, and full of trouble.

Job 23:10: But He knoweth the way I take: when He hath tried me, I shall come forth as gold.

Proverbs 3:5-6: Trust in the Lord with all thine heart; and lean not unto thine own understanding. In all thine ways acknowledge Him, and He shall direct thy paths.

Romans 8:28: And we know that all things work together for good to them that love God, to them who are the called according to His purpose.

Psalm 33:5: He loveth righteousness and judgment: the earth is full of the goodness of the Lord.

Chapter 17

Run Towards a New Beginning and Away From a Guilty Conscience and Depression Can Be Removed

Every day we live we should live life to its fullest. Jesus intends for us to have joy unspeakable and full of glory. The Bible says that God wants us to have life and have it more abundantly. Each day should be filled with excitement, energy, goals, dreams, and achievements. Psalm 118:24 says "This is the day which the Lord hath made; we will rejoice and be glad in it". David said "My cup runneth over and thou hast given me fullness of joy". What's so sad about depression is that the Devil keeps us bound up with the same guilt over and over and over again and instead of enjoying life we are content staying in our comfort zone and we never grow for God. The Devil is a master at messing with us, and running the same guilt over and over again through our minds like a broken record to the point of it driving us insane. We cannot enjoy anything God has for us because we allow Satan to beat us up with guilt and disgrace. If Satan can depress us he knows we will not be productive and we will be useless in our everyday life. Paul said in Philippians Ch. 3:13 "Brethren, I count not myself to have apprehended: but this one thing I do, forgetting those things which are behind, and reaching forth unto those things which are before". Paul is saying in this verse that it's impossible to live the victorious Christian life if we never move passed the guilt of yesterday. I've seen people stand up in tent revivals and say things like this "Tonight I got victory over a sin that has haunted me for 35 years". It's scary to think that one thought of guilt can be replayed in our minds every day for 35 years but it's happening all over this world.

A great preacher once said this and I've never forgotten it: "Christ has forgiven you, learn to forgive yourself". If the same thought haunts you day in and day out the Bible is clear that this degree of confusion can only come from one place and it isn't God. The Bible says that "God is not the author of confusion"; but Satan is. Whatever haunts you, take that thing to the Lord and leave it there. If Satan tries to bring it up again remind yourself it's under the blood and you have been forgiven. Don't go days, weeks, months, or years reliving the same thought over and over again. Get rid of that mindset and you can experience a new start. Make each second count for God because we are not promised tomorrow. Tell Satan that you're done listening to his lies and refuse to live in your past anymore. Experience victory, anointing, and the power of a new beginning through the freedom of a renewed mind. Go forward, not backwards, and you can avoid depression.

Scriptures -- Chapter Seventeen

Psalm 118:24: This is the day which the Lord hath made; well will rejoice and be glad in it.

Philippians 3:13: Brethren, I count not myself to have apprehended: but this one thing I do, forgetting those things which are behind; and reaching forth unto those things which are before.

I Corinthians 14:33: For God is not the author of confusion, but of peace, as in the churches of the Saints.

John 10:10: The thief cometh not, but for to steal, and to kill, and to destroy: I am come that they might have life, and that they might have it more abundantly.

Chapter 18

You Must Run to Total Faith If You Want Depression to be Taken Care Of

When we come to Jesus for healing we must come to Him in total faith or nothing will ever happen. We cannot come with doubt, or He will not respond to our plead for help. All throughout the ministry of Jesus Christ people came to Him desperate and longing for the Master to show mercy on their broken condition. Jesus would often ask them if they believed He could and if they responded in total faith He would touch them. The Bible still says in Hebrews 13:8 "Jesus Christ the same yesterday, today, and forever" and He is still looking to respond to those who have absolute confidence in His ability to heal. The Bible says in Mark 9:23 "Jesus said unto him, if thou can't believe, all things are possible to him that believeth". Jesus can still heal anyone in depression but it will not come to pass if we doubt that He can. The Bible says in Hebrews 11:6 "But without faith it is impossible to please Him: for he that cometh to God must believe that He is, and that He is a rewarder of them that diligently seek Him". God is able to do anything but we tie His hands, spiritually speaking, when we doubt His abilities. The Bible says in Ephesians 3:20 that God is able to do things that we cannot even comprehend so He is not the problem – we are. The Bible says in Matthew 19:26 "But Jesus beheld them, and said unto them, with men this is impossible: but with God all things are possible". If we will just reach out and grab the hem of His garment in total faith we could get much needed relief from whatever afflicts us. Jesus always responds to those who believe Him, and He can set you free from the bondage of depression. Matthew 9:22 says "But Jesus turned him about, and when he saw her, he said Daughter, be of good comfort, thy faith hath made thee whole". If you are hurting, don't let anyone stop you from getting to Jesus today. Always remember that a million people can say your situation is hopeless but one word from Jesus can make all the difference.

We serve a God who can walk on the water, still the raging sea, and can set the sinner free. There is no reason to doubt such a powerful God. If you are in chains of darkness, run to Him today. Your depression can melt away with just three simple words from Jesus: "Peace Be Still". Total faith in God is always the answer to any problem we face, but it is up to us to respond in belief and if we will all things are possible. Matthew 28:18 still says "And Jesus came and spake unto them, saying, all power is given unto me in Heaven and in earth". Jesus has the power to cure any problem you bring to Him by faith but we must make the first step. If we will move towards God He will move towards us with healing in His wings. Trust in God's power to deliver you and He can cast your mountain of depression into the deepest sea by His Amazing Grace. Matthew 17:20 says "And Jesus said unto them, if ye have faith as a grain of mustard seed, ye shall say unto this mountain, remove hence to yonder place; and it shall remove, and nothing shall be impossible unto you". Just a measure of faith can take you from the depths of woe to heights you have never known. All it takes is faith and your depression can be blotted out by the mighty hand of God.

Scriptures -- Chapter Eighteen

Hebrews 13:8: Jesus Christ the same yesterday, today, and forever.

Mark 9:23: Jesus said unto him, if thou can't believe, all things are possible to him that believeth.

Hebrews 11:6: But without faith it is impossible to please Him: for he that cometh to God must believe that He is, and that He is a rewarder of them that diligently seek Him.

Matthew 19:26: But Jesus beheld them, and said unto them, with men this is impossible: but with God all things are possible.

Matthew 9:22: But Jesus turned him about, and when he saw her, he said Daughter, be of good comfort, thy faith hath made thee whole.

Matthew 28:18: And Jesus came and spake unto them, saying, all power is given unto me in Heaven and in earth.

Matthew 17:20: And Jesus said unto them, ye have faith as a grain of mustard seed, ye shall say unto this mountain, remove hence to yonder place; and it shall remove, and nothing shall be impossible unto you.

Chapter 19

Whenever You Are Depressed, Deep Bible Study Works

One of the greatest preachers that ever lived said this and I quote "I would rather have a vast knowledge of the Bible than to have every degree from every secular college, knowing the Bible is of a far greater value". Anytime depression arises in our lives we need to run to the Bible for help and relief. The Bible says study to show thyself approved unto God. The art of study and knowing God's Word is really missing in people's lives and when depression hits them they sink in the mire instead of standing on the rock. If you know the Bible inside and out it will be far easier to deal with depression because you will know where to run when life begins to crumble.

The Bible has all the answers but we must study them to know what they are. The Bible says in Psalm 119:130 "The entrance of thy words giveth light. It giveth understanding unto the simple". If you're in darkness and you feel like you're spiritual feet are in quicksand, open up the Word of God and get some help. Psalm 119:18 says "Open thou mine eyes, that I may behold wondrous things out of thy law". If Satan is blinding you, open up God's law and you will begin to see clearly again. The Bible says in Psalm Ch. 1:1-3 "Blessed is the man that walketh not in the council of the ungodly, nor standeth in the ways of sinners, nor sitteth in the seat of the scornful. But his delight is in the law of the Lord; and in His law doth he mediate day and night. And he shall be like a tree planted by the rivers of water, that bringeth forth fruit in his season; His leaf also shall not wither; and whatsoever he doeth shall prosper". If you want to be blessed you must know God's Word. If you have a desire to grow you must mediate on His word. If you want to be prosperous you must study God's word. Everyone I've ever known who has had a vast knowledge of God's word are strong, mature, and joyful in their walk with God. Knowing God's Word will stop depression from growing in our lives. Isaiah 26:3 says we can have perfect peace if our minds are stayed on Him. The Bible commands us to give attendance to reading and if we don't Satan will gain an advantage over us. Jesus said this in Matthew 22:29 "Ye do err, not knowing the Scriptures nor the power of God". Jesus called out those who were just carrying a Bible and were not living it. Jesus told the Pharisees that they looked good on the outside but on the inside they were filled with dead men's bones. As Jesus looks over society today He sees the same quality in people. The Bible says in the last days knowledge would increase but true understanding of God's Word would decrease and people as a whole would be weak and defeated. The Bible says in the last days people would be destroyed for lack of knowledge in God's Word. The Bible says there would be a great famine of God's Word and depression and sorrow would grow.

Paul said God wants us to be strong Christians and without knowing God's Word that is impossible. The more we forsake God's Word the more demonic oppression will increase in our lives. The Bible says in Hebrews 4:12 "For the Word of God is quick, and powerful, and sharper than any two edged sword". When a Christian is strong in the Word he will be able to defend himself against Satan. People in America are consumed with everything except a knowledge of God's Word and it's killing them and they don't even realize it. Knowing God's Word is so important and we need to take it very seriously if we want to ward off depression.

Jesus gave us the formula to overcome depression in Matthew Ch. 4 and Luke Ch. 4 and this formula works every time. When Christ was being tempted by Satan in the wilderness, He battled him through prayer, fasting, and the Word of God. After a 40 day battle with the Devil the Bible is clear that Jesus was the winner and Luke 4:14 says this "And Jesus returned in the power of the Spirit in to Galilee: and there went out a fame of Him through all the region round about Him". After His temptation Jesus did more miracles than He did before the battle with Satan and He showed by example that if you increase in God's Word the Devil must flee. Matthew Ch. 4:4 says "It is written men shall not live by bread alone, but by every Word that proceedeth out of the mouth of God". We must make the Bible our life, not just a part of our life. Every time we read God's word it will be profitable to us. The Bible says in II Timothy 3:16 "All Scripture is given by inspiration of God, and is profitable for doctrine, for reproof, for correction, for instruction in righteousness". Every time we read the Bible we will grow. I Peter 2:2 says "As newborn babes, desire the sincere milk of the Word, that ye may grow thereby". Psalm 138:2 says "For thou hast magnified thy Word above all thy name". If you will dive into the Word of God, the Lord can remove your depression and make you strong like a lion. The Bible says "Trust ye in the Lord forever: for in the Lord Jehovah is everlasting strength".

The next time Satan tries to make you feel weak, run towards God's Word and He can make you strong. The Bible says "The Lord is my rock, and my fortress, and my deliverer; my God, my strength, in whom I will trust; my buckler, and the horn of my salvation, and my high tower". Psalm 119:32 says "I will run the way of thy commandments, when thou shalt enlarge my heart". When depression is all around it's always best to run to God's Word for the remedy. The Bible says "Great peace have they which love thy law: and nothing shall offend them". Study God's Word, and mediate on God's word and your depression will turn into great peace.

Thank the Lord for the precious Word of God and for the power it has to set the captive free.

Scriptures -- Chapter Nineteen

Psalm 119:130: The entrance of thy words giveth light: it giveth understanding unto the simple.

Psalm 119:18: Open thou mine eyes, that I may behold wondrous things out of thy law.

Psalm 1:1-3: Blessed is thy man that walketh not in the council of the ungodly, nor standeth in the ways of sinners, nor sitteth in the seat of the scornful. But his delight is in the law of the Lord; and in His law doth he mediate day and night. And he shall be like a tree planted by the rivers of water, that bringeth forth fruit in his season; his leaf also shall not wither; and whatsoever he doeth shall prosper.

Isaiah 26:3: Thou wilt keep him in perfect peace, whose mind is stayed on thee: because he trusteth in thee.

Matthew 22:29: Jesus answered and said unto them, ye do err, not knowing the Scriptures, nor the power of God.

Luke 4:14: And Jesus returned in the power of the Spirit into Galilee: and there went out a fame of Him through all the region round about Him.

Matthew 4:4: It is written men shall not live by bread alone, but by every Word that proceedeth out of the mouth of God.

II Timothy 3:16: All Scripture is given by inspiration of God, and is profitable for doctrine, for reproof, for correction, for instruction in righteousness.

I Peter 2:2: As newborn babes, desire the sincere milk of the Word, that ye may grow thereby.

Psalm 138:2: For thou hast magnified thy Word above all thy name.

Isaiah 26:4: Trust in the Lord forever: for in the Lord Jehovah is everlasting strength.

Psalm 18:2: The Lord is my rock, and my fortress, and my deliverer; my strength, in whom I trust; my buckler, and the horn of my salvation, and my high tower.

Psalm 119:32: I will run the way of thy commandments, when thou shalt enlarge my heart.

Psalm 119:165: Great peace have they that love thy law: and nothing shall offend them.

II Timothy 2:15: Study to show thyself approved unto God, a workman that needeth not to be ashamed, rightly divi

Chapter 20

Live a Busy and Productive Life and You Can Cut Down Depression

When a person spends their life being active and busy it will give them less time to be consumed with worry, fear, and depression. The Bible says in Luke 9:62 "And Jesus said unto him, no man, having put his hand to the plough, and looking back, is fit for the Kingdom of God". We are living in days of extreme laziness and as a result depression has become common in many people's lives. In Proverbs Ch. 6 the Bible tells us to watch the ant and take notes on how active they are and how productive their existence is. The ant works day and night and is always productive. As long as people stay in the fight and have a mind to work depression will not control their life.

The Bible teaches that King David was a special force and constantly throughout his life he worked hard, won battles, and was productive. As long as David stayed busy, his life was blessed, and his steps were ordered by the Lord. The

Bible teaches that one day David decided to skip a battle he was supposed to fight in and this decision came back to bite him over and over again. With free time on his hands and no accountability, David's eyes, heart, and mind started to wander after a righteous man's wife and David decided to obey his flesh more than fearing his God. David took this woman for himself and secretly had an affair with her and it caused judgement and depression to show up on David's front door. As a result of David's sin he murdered a man to try to cover his sin, four of his kids died, and the sword of judgement never left his house. This decision to get out of the fight cost David his joy, peace, blessings, and he felt like he wanted to die as guilt and shame entered his life. The Bible says in Psalm Ch. 51 that David was broken and begged God for his joy back and he asked for forgiveness because he couldn't live another moment in depression.

    I've always been trained that the idle mind is the Devil's playground. Stay active, work hard, and spend your time and energy thinking on God, not your problems. The Lord Jesus Christ was always doing a miracle, working, preaching, helping others, laboring, praying, travelling, and healing. Jesus made the statement "I must be about my Father's business". Christ is our great example and if He spend His life active and busy we must follow His same pattern. God blesses those who are busy and seems to curse those who are lazy. Proverbs Ch. 20:4 says "The sluggard shall not plow by reason of the cold: therefore shall he beg in harvest, and have nothing". The Bible still says "That if any would not work neither should he eat". The Bible says we should labor all our days, and have a vision to reach the world. God did not create us to sit around in depression, He designed us to be busy, productive, and fruitful increasing in wisdom, strength, and favor with Him. The Bible says we are to grow in grace and we are supposed to be the salt of the earth and the light of the world.

If you are busy in life God can bless your life, direct your steps, and He can keep your mind fresh in a positive way. Anyone who has made a real difference in life has done it through hard work. When we are busy about the Master's work, we have no time for the Devil's lies. Much like David, people get in a mess when their minds begin to wander and their hands begin to relax. Millions around this world lay around defeated because they have just given up and they allow Satan to control their life instead of God. Depression stops progress in anyone's life and it becomes very dangerous and very fatal. We must fight Satan, and refuse to just sit back and let him take over. We must fight hard, work hard, and serve hard if we want to accomplish greatness in life. God will bless all those who labor for Him with rewards, blessings, and peace of mind. Many could escape depression if they would just get up, get active, and work for God. You cannot just sit around and allow Satan to torture your mind. Get busy doing God's work and your life, mind, and attitude will improve. Spend more energy working than worrying and depression will run and hide from you. The Bible says in I Corinthians 15:57-58 "But thanks be to God, which giveth us the victory through our Lord Jesus Christ. Therefore my beloved brethren, be steadfast, unmovable, always abounding in the work of the Lord, for as much as ye know that your labor is not in vain in the Lord". Work hard all your days for the Lord and you will make a difference. Don't be content to live in the state of depression because it will steal your time, energy, joy, and happiness. Get up, dust yourself off, and give God your life and you too can make a difference in other's lives.

Scriptures -- Chapter Twenty

Luke 9:62: And Jesus said unto him, no man having put his hand to the plough, and looking back is fit for the Kingdom of God.

Psalm 51:10: Create in me a clean heart, O God; and renew a right spirit within me.

Proverbs 20:4: The sluggard shall not plow by reason of the cold: therefore shall he beg in harvest, and have nothing.

I Corinthians 15:58: Therefore my beloved brethren, be ye steadfast, unmovable, always abounding in the work of the Lord, for as much as ye know that your labor is not in vain in the Lord.

Chapter 21

If You Are in Depression, Run Towards Spirit-Filled Preaching

There is only one kind of preaching that gets the job done when it comes to delivering people from depression and that is Spirit-filled preaching. When Jesus started His ministry, thousands in depression thronged Jesus and begged Him for help because they knew He had the power to heal. The Bible says in Luke 4:18 "The Spirit of the Lord is upon me, because He hath anointed me to preach the Gospel to the poor: He hath sent me to heal the broken hearted, to preach deliverance to the captives, and recovering of sight to the blind, to set at liberty them that are bruised". Those who were afflicted with demons and thoughts of depression always ran to Jesus for help and never ran to the scribes and ministers who had no power from On High. There was a huge difference between Jesus preaching and the ministers of those days dead preaching. When people walked away from Christ's message they always got help whereas when they left the priests and ministers message they left worse than they came. If you're suffering from depression run to Spirit-filled preaching and you will find answers to your problems.

The Bible tells us about a woman in Luke 13 that was bound by Satan for 18 long years and no one could help her. She had heard message after message and never got any help. The Bible says she had a spirit of infirmity and she was bound by her infirmity. The Bible records that one encounter with a Spirit-filled preacher made the difference and the ruler of the Synagogue was mad because Jesus healed on the Sabbath Day.

If you are suffering from depression, don't just go to any church to hear any preacher. Get in a place where God's power is real and deliverance is possible. The Bible says in Acts 10:38 "How God anointed Jesus of Nazareth with the Holy Ghost and with Power: who went about doing good, and healing all that were oppressed of the Devil; for God was with Him". If you're oppressed by the Devil, get around Spirit-filled preaching because any other kind of preaching just won't work. When people are captured with depression, cute little sermons won't help and they will never bring change. People in depression need power from On High to break the bondage that surrounds them and God will use Spirit-filled preaching to do it. When I young I went through a valley of depression that nearly destroyed me and nothing would help. Preacher after preacher delivered messages but nothing worked. This lasted for about 15 months and as I was about to give up God sent a man my way that preached with a power from another world and I hit an altar and the depression went away. God uses Spirit-filled preaching to minister to the hurting and it's the only preaching that works. Jesus would not even send out His Disciples in the Book of Acts until they were endued with power from On High. After God's anointing fell on them they began to preach, perform miracles, and they turned the world upside down. Depression will not go away when preachers deliver powerless sermons, but it will when men preach with power.

One thing that really helped me keep depression at bay was a decision to buy 140 preaching tapes from a Spirit-filled man of God. Within two months I listened to all those tapes and my depression left me and hasn't returned. There is something about anointed preaching that delivers those who are struggling. Paul said in I Corinthian 2:4 "And my speech and preaching was not with enticing words of man's wisdom, but in demonstration of the Spirit and of power". God's power must be present to deliver those in depression and without it deliverance will never happen. If you are desperate for help, search for Spirit-filled preaching and I promise it can rescue you like it did me. It's difficult to find powerful preaching in these days but search for it like hidden treasure and you can find comfort. The Bible says in Luke 4:1 "And Jesus being full of the Holy Ghost returned from Jordan, and was led by the Spirit into the wilderness". Find preaching that is full of the Holy Ghost and has the power to heal you from the awful feeling of depression. Without Spirit-filled preaching I would probably still be in depression, but thank God for the grace of Almighty God. An encounter with powerful preaching can change your life forever, and your spirit can be renewed for His Kingdom.

Scriptures -- Chapter Twenty-One

Luke 4:18: The Spirit of the Lord is upon me, because He hath anointed me to preach the Gospel to the poor: He hath sent me to heal the broken hearted, to preach deliverance to the captives, and recovering of sight to the blind, to set at liberty them that are bruised.

Acts 10:38: How God anointed Jesus of Nazareth with the Holy Ghost and with Power: who went about doing good, and healing all that were oppressed of the Devil; for God was with Him.

I Corinthians 2:4: And my speech and preaching was not enticing words of man's wisdom, but in demonstration of the Spirit and of the power.

Luke 4:1: And Jesus being full of the Holy Ghost returned from Jordan, and was led by the Spirit into the wilderness.

Chapter 22

Run Towards Positive People When You Are Depressed

The key to running any race is to shed any weight that may hinder your chances of winning or being successful. In Hebrews Ch. 12:1 the Bibles says "Wherefore seeing we also are compassed about with so great a cloud of witnesses, let us lay aside every weight, and the sin which doth so easily beset us, and let us run with patience the race that is set before us". Being around negative people will slow us down and drain us of so much joy and replace it with depression. I've seen so many people fall short of their dreams because they allowed negative people to derail them from their ultimate goal. Many athletes, movie stars, Saints, pastors, and people in general are tormented by depression because they have been hurt by some person and it's caused them to lose focus and they carry baggage of regret and guilt with them every day. Never allow negative people to weigh you down and stop you from your goals and dreams. Get around as many positive people as you can who will encourage you to go another mile. Depression will intensify around negativity and it's wise to eliminate hurtful people from your life. The older I'm getting the more I realize that if I get around people who love me the world is a better place. Stop allowing people to hurt you, and refuse to be around anyone who finds ways to discourage you. The last thing you want to do when you're feeling down is to hang out with others who are down as well. Get around those who lift you up and will offer help and your depression will improve. Negative people are like heavy chains around your ankles and to walk for God will seem impossible. The Bible teaches us to be disciplined, serious, and trained in the things of God. Use wisdom as you pick your friends because those you choose will affect your life both good and bad. Run to those with a loving and caring spirit and run far away from anyone who never tries to help.

The key to getting out of depression is to have a great support team. The Bible says "Have no fellowship with the unfruitful works of darkness". If you are depressed, drop the weights that hold you down and get around those who will make you believe you can spread your wings and fly again. When people are supporting us we feel like we can do anything. Fill your mind with positive thoughts and your life with positive people. If you will get rid of negative people your load will be lighter and your race will be easier to run.

Scriptures -- Chapter Twenty-Two

Hebrews 12:1: Wherefore seeing we also are compassed about with so great a cloud of witnesses, let us lay aside every weight, and the sin which doth so easily beset us, and let us run with patience the race that is set before us.

Ephesians 5:11: And have no fellowship with the unfruitful works of darkness, but rather reprove them.

Chapter 23

When Depression Hits You, Drop What You're Doing and Run to the Blood of Jesus

The greatest advice I could ever give anyone suffering from depression is to run to the blood of Jesus as fast as you can. Nothing strikes fear in the heart of Satan or his demons more than the blood does. Whenever you feel overwhelmed with guilt, ashamed, defeated, dirty, and filthy, run to the fountain filled with blood and you can be clean from head to toe. I John 1:7 declares "But if we walk in the light, as He is in the light, we have fellowship one with another, and the blood of Jesus Christ His son cleanseth us from all sin". It does not matter what fear has a hold of you, the blood can set you free. It does not matter what you have done or whom you have been, the blood can wash you whiter than snow, and make you whole. The Bible says in Revelation 1:5 "Unto Him that loved us and washed us from our sins in His own blood". The old song says "There is a fountain filled with blood, drawn from Emmanuel's veins, and sinners plunged beneath that flood lose all their guilty stains. If you're depressed, saturate your life with songs about the blood, preaching about the blood, and thoughts about the blood and Satan will run from you and depression will run with him. Colossians 1:14 says "In whom we have redemption through His blood, even the forgiveness of sins". The blood of Jesus can bring forgiveness to any sinner and bring you joy on the inside. Colossians 1:20 says "And having made peace through the blood of His cross, by Him to reconcile all things to Himself: by Him I say, whether they be things in earth or things in Heaven". The blood of Jesus can clean up your mind, cleanse your soul, and brighten your future. The Bible says in I John 1:9 "If we confess our sins, He is faithful and just to forgive us our sins, and to cleanse us from all unrighteous".

If you are tired of feeling depressed and defeated the blood of Jesus is the answer for it can give you a brand new start. I Corinthians Ch 6:9-11 says this "Knew ye not that the unrighteous shall not inherit the Kingdom of God? Be not deceived, neither fornicators, nor idolaters, nor adulterers, nor effeminate, nor abusers of themselves with mankind, nor thieves, nor coveters, nor drunkards, nor revilers, nor extortioners, shall inherit the Kingdom of God. And such were some of you: but ye are washed, but ye are sanctified, but you are justified in the name of the Lord Jesus, and by the Spirit of our God". Without the blood we will always be miserable but through the blood we are forgiven, and clean in God's sight. Satan cannot handle the blood and when we make much about the blood Satan will choose someone else to bother. Every time you feel vile and unclean just run to that fountain filled with blood and you will feel like a newborn baby all over again. The blood of Jesus has the power to break any chain that binds you and it will remove depression from your life. There is something within the heart of every human that longs to be clean and the blood of Jesus can cleanse every stain. The third verse of There is a Fountain reads like this "E'er since by faith I saw the stream, thy flowing wounds supply, redeeming love has been my theme, and shall be 'til I die". If we can make these words the theme of our life we can walk in total victory and we can kiss depression goodbye.

Thank God for that fountain filled with blood that causes Satan and his demons to run every time. When you're in trouble just claim the blood and depression will scramble in fear.

Scriptures -- Chapter Twenty-Three

I John 1:7: But if we walk in the light, as He is in the light, we have fellowship one with another, and the blood of Jesus Christ His son cleanseth us from all sin.

Revelation 1:5: Unto Him that loved us, and washed us from our sins in His own blood.

Colossians 1:14: In whom we have redemption through His blood, even the forgiveness of sins.

Colossians 1:20: And having made peace through the blood of His cross, by Him to reconcile all things to Himself: by Him I say, whether they be things in earth or things in Heaven.

I John 1:9: If we confess our sins, He is faithful and just to forgive us our sins, and to cleanse us from all unrighteousness.

I Corinthians 6:9-11: Know ye not that the unrighteous shall not inherit the Kingdom of God? Be not deceived, neither fornicators, nor idolaters, nor adulterers, nor effeminate, nor abusers of themselves with mankind, nor thieves, nor coveters, nor drunkards, nor revilers, nor extortioners, shall inherit the Kingdom of God. And such were some of you: but ye are washed, but ye are sanctified, but you are justified in the name of the Lord Jesus, and by the Spirit of our God.

CONCLUSION

As we close out this book I want to express to you how much I love you and how much I appreciate you reading this book. My heart breaks for the millions battling with depression and I pray that this book provided answers from the Word of God.

Before we completely close out this book I just want to point out that there are some cases that involve chemical imbalances and if medication is helping you, please don't stop taking it. There are some cases where medicine is the only thing that helps, but I'm a strong believer that in most cases God has the answers to all of the questions we have. God never designed for anyone to live in a prison of fear and if you come to Him in faith He can come to your side with help straight from His throne. The Bible says in Hebrews 4:15 "For we have not a high priest which cannot be touched with the feeling of our infirmities; but was in all points tempted like as we are, yet without sin". There is nothing that you and I will ever go through that God does not understand. God loves you and His whole purpose in coming to earth was to set the captive free. If you will turn to Jesus today, He can change your life, redeem your soul, and give you a whole different life. Hebrews 12:2 says "Looking unto Jesus the author and finisher of our faith; who for the joy that was set before Him endured the cross, despising the shame, and is set down at the right hand of the throne of God". Revelation 22;17 says "And the Spirit and the bride say come, and let him that heareth say come, and let him that is a thirst come, and whosoever will, let him take of the water of life freely". If you are tired of being depressed come to Jesus and He will give you rest. Matthew 11:28 says "Come unto me, all ye that labor and are heavy laden and I will give you rest".

The Bible says "Behold, I stand at the door, and knock: if any man hear my voice, and open the door, I will come in to him, and will sup with him, and he with me". Time is running out and life is swiftly passing by. You would be wise today to trade your chains of depression for a white robe of righteousness. By the authority of God's word you can leave the darkness and step into the light. Jesus said "I am the way, the truth, and the life; no man cometh unto the Father but by me". God has a beautiful new future just waiting for you but you must leave Satan to get it. The Bible says "For the wages of sin is death: but the gift of God is eternal life through Jesus Christ our Lord". Jesus offers eternal life to any and all who will reach out and receive it. The Bible says in John 8:32 "And ye shall know the truth, and the truth shall make you free".

Come to Jesus and He can turn your frown upside down. You can leave your past behind through the blood of Jesus Christ. The Bible says "As far as the East is from the West, so far hath He removed our transgressions from us". All the guilt you carry, and all the pain you feel can be cast into the deepest sea. Let Jesus take away your heavy burden and replace it with a home on high. Jesus said he that cometh to me I will in no wise cast out.

You have a promise from God today and He cannot lie but it's up to you to accept this free gift of salvation. What will you do with Jesus Christ?

Luke 4:18
Bro Tony

Scriptures -- Conclusion

Hebrews 4:15: For we have not a high priest which cannot be touched with the feeling of our infirmities; but was in all points tempted like as we are, yet without sin.

Hebrews 12:2: Looking unto Jesus the author and finisher of our faith; who for the joy that was set before Him endured the cross, despising the shame, and is set down at the right hand of the throne of God.

Revelation 22:17: And the Spirit and the bride say come, and let him that heareth say come, and let him that is a thirst come, and whosoever will, let him take of the water of life freely.

John 8:32: And ye shall know the truth, and the truth shall make you free.

John 14:6: I am the way, the truth, and the life; no man cometh unto the Father but by me.

ANTHONY RITTHALER

Published By Parables

OUR MISSION

The primary mission of Published By Parables, a Christian publisher, is to publish Contemporary and Classic Christian books from an evangelical perspective that honors Christ and promotes the values and virtues of His Kingdom.

Are You An Aspiring Christian Author?

We fulfill our mission best by providing Christian authors and writers publishing options that are uniquely Christian, quick, affordable and easy to understand -- in an effort to please Christ who has called us to a writing ministry. We know the challenges of getting published, especially if you're a first-time author. God, who called you to write your book, will provide the grace sufficient to the task of getting it published.

We understand the value of a dollar; know the importance of producing a quality product; and publish what we publish for the glory of God.

Surf and Explore our site --
then use our easy-to-use "Tell Us" button
to tell us about yourself and about your book.

We're a one-stop, full-service Christian publisher.
We know our limits. We know our capabilities.
You won't be disappointed.

www.PublishedByParables.com

ANTHONY RITTHALER

Escaping Depression

ANTHONY RITTHALER

www.ingramcontent.com/pod-product-compliance
Lightning Source LLC
Chambersburg PA
CBHW071740080526
44588CB00013B/2101